NATIONAL
GEOGRAPHIC

My Town at Work

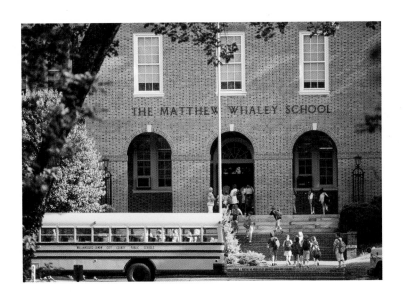

Gare Thompson

Contents

Where do you live? Do you live in a big city? Or do you live in a small town? Who makes the laws? How do things get done?

I live in a small town. I like my town. There are lots of things to do here.

Come with me on a tour of my town. We'll see public buildings and parks. We'll meet the people who work for the town. And we'll meet the people who run the town. Let's go. Come find out about my town and how it works.

Chapter 1

Public Places

The Library

Our first stop is the public library. I have some books to return. I show my library card and I get to check out books for free.

Our library also has videos, tapes, and DVDs. You can find almost any kind of information at the library. The librarians help me find books for school reports. They also help me find books to read for fun.

Some groups hold meetings at the library. Some people use the computers to search the Internet. Our neighbor, Mr. Diaz, goes there to read the paper.

Schools

Now let's go to my school. My school has grades kindergarten to fifth grade. When I start the sixth grade, I will go to the middle school. I'll be there through eighth grade.

I will start high school in ninth grade. The high school in my town is old. We need a new building. The people in the town will vote to decide if money should be spent to build a new high school. I hope most people vote yes.

The Senior Center

Let's go to the senior center. The senior center is where many older people in town go during the day. My grandmother is a **senior citizen**. She goes to the center most days.

There are many things for seniors to do at the center. They take classes, play games, and see friends there. My grandmother is taking a drawing class. Sometimes, she goes on day trips with other people from the senior center. They visit museums or go to see shows.

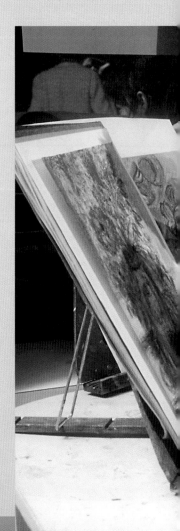

My grandmother and other people at the senior center know a lot about our town. I am giving a report about our town to my class. The seniors are going to help me. They are telling me what our town was like long ago. I like their stories.

Our senior center is new. The town got money from the state to build it. It's a nice place for the seniors to get together. Now, some people are talking about trying to get money to build a teen center. Many teenagers would like that. We do have a new playground. Let's go there next.

Parks

My town has many parks. People ride their bikes, eat lunch, or sit and read in the parks. Children play on the playgrounds. The parks and recreation department takes care of the parks and playgrounds. In the summer, workers in the department plan programs for the town. There are concerts, games, and camps. On July 4, there's a big fireworks display.

Our town used to have just one playground. It was very crowded. My family and some other families worked hard to get the town to build a new playground. We started a **campaign**. We talked to people who owned stores near the park where we wanted the new playground. We told them how a new playground would help business. Stores could advertise in the park. The store owners gave money to help build the new playground.

Then we took the idea to the **town council**.
We explained why the playground was a good idea.
Many people supported us. Some people wrote letters
to the local paper. Others came to a **town meeting**.
The town council voted to build the new playground.

Chapter 2

Keeping Safe

The Hospital

The hospital is the place where people in my town go for medical care. People from other towns also use our hospital. It is a good one. We have fine doctors and nurses. I don't want to be sick, but if I am, this is a good place to be.

My aunt works at the hospital. She is a nurse. She helps care for people in the hospital. She has many important jobs. Sometimes she feeds patients who cannot feed themselves.

My sister wants to be a doctor. She is a **volunteer** at our local hospital. She reads to the patients. She also takes them for walks and talks to them.

Emergency Workers

My town has emergency workers. They ride in the ambulances. These workers are trained to care for sick and injured people. They know CPR. This helps people stay alive when they are badly hurt.

One day, our neighbor was sick. He needed help. He called 911. This is the number you call when there is an emergency and you need help. The ambulance came very fast. The workers took care of him. They rushed him to the hospital. Then the doctors and nurses took over. He says that the emergency workers saved his life.

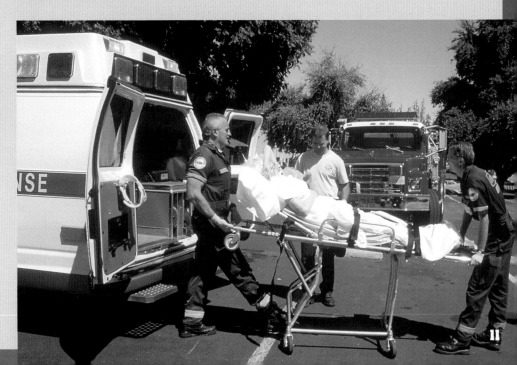

The Fire Department

The fire chief is in charge of the fire department. Both full-time and volunteer firefighters work for the fire department. Being a firefighter is hard work.

Our firefighters are well trained. They often go to school to learn new things. They need to know how to use new equipment. But most importantly, they must be ready to go to a fire quickly.

A horn blares. You hear sirens. The firefighters are on their way to a fire. Some firefighters work the engine truck. They set up the hoses and pumps. They spray water onto the fire. Other firefighters work the ladder truck. The ladder is tall. Firefighters use it to reach the top of buildings and to rescue people.

The Police

We have a small police department. The chief of police is the head of the police department. The other police officers work with the chief. There are police officers on duty all the time. They work different **shifts**, or periods of time.

The police do many things to keep us safe. They patrol our town. When people see the police they feel safe. They know that the police are here to help us.

Our police use both cars and bikes. Some police cars have flashing lights. They also have sirens. When we see the lights flash and hear the sirens we know the police need to get somewhere fast or want to stop someone.

The police are in charge of keeping our roadways safe. They stop speeders. They have radar in their cars. The radar tells how fast a car is going. A driver who gets a speeding ticket has to pay a **fine**.

Sometimes police officers come to our school. They talk to us about how to be safe. My friend, Sara, wants to be a police officer. She likes the idea of helping people.

Chapter 3

Getting Around

Walking and Biking

My town has lots of sidewalks for walking. The traffic lights and stop signs help keep us safe when we walk. Streetlights are lit at night to help us see where we are going.

The town put in a new traffic light in front of our school last year. Some of the older students campaigned to get one there. The students spoke to the town council. They said that many kids had trouble crossing the street after school. Drivers did not always stop. With the new light, drivers have to stop so that kids can cross the road safely.

We have bike paths in our town. Many people ride their bikes to work. This helps keep our air clean. My family likes to go to the park on weekends. We all take our bikes and ride on the paths. I like the path that goes around the lake. I like to stop and feed the ducks. So does my Dad.

Public Transportation

My father takes the bus to work. He gets on the bus at the bus stop by our house. The bus follows the same **route** every day. The bus stops to pick up many people who are also going into town. My friends and I sometimes take the bus, too.

There is a special bus for the senior citizens. They pay a special price. It picks them up at the senior center. It takes them shopping and then back to the center. The bus has big letters on it saying it is the bus for seniors.

There is a lot of roadwork going on in my town this year. The town got some money from the state to build and repair roads. We are adding another lane to the main road going to town center. Other workers are repaving roads to get rid of the potholes. Police direct traffic around the roadwork. They make sure the workers and the drivers are safe.

Chapter 4

A Visit to Town Hall

Paying Town Bills

Our last stop is Town Hall. Many things happen here. The town council meets in this building. The **mayor** and her staff have offices here. People come here to get **licenses** and other important papers.

My best friend's dad is opening a new restaurant in town. He went to Town Hall to get permission to open his restaurant. He showed them his plans and got permission to open a restaurant. Then he paid a fee for his business license.

Do you know how we pay for all the different **services** we have in town? Well, **taxes** pay for most of them. All of the people in town who own property pay taxes. These taxes are used to pay for a lot of things. The town clerk collects the taxes.

Our taxes pay for the teachers and the librarians. Taxes also pay for the people who take care of the parks and pick up the trash. They pay for the firefighters and the police.

Meet the Mayor

The person who runs our town is the mayor. The people of the town vote for the person they think will be the best mayor. The people who want to be mayor campaign for the job. They give speeches and put up posters telling what they will do for the town.

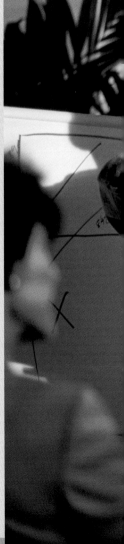

There was an **election** last November. The man who had been mayor did not run again. The voters elected a new mayor. She is my mom!

The town council helps the mayor run the town. Each council member is elected from a different part of town. The town council discusses and then votes on town issues and laws.

There are other groups of people that help run our town, too. The finance committee advises the town council about taxes and spending money. The school board helps run the schools.

Well, this is my town. Is it like your town? Or is it different? No matter where you live, it's important that you know how your town or city is run. Pitch in and help! You can make your town or city a better place.

Glossary

campaign	a set of activities done for a certain result
election	the process of choosing people for jobs by voting
fine	an amount of money that someone must pay as a penalty
license	a permit that allows a person to own or operate something
mayor	the elected leader of a town
route	a path or line of travel
senior citizen	an older member of a community
services	functions, such as police protection, that a town provides for its citizens
shift	the period of time that a person works at a job
taxes	charges that a town, state, or country require citizens to pay
town council	a group of people that are elected to make decisions for other people in the town
town meeting	a gathering of people that is led by the town council
volunteer	a person who gives his or her time to a group or organization without being paid